Into My Eyes Poetry

Anna Elizabeth, Jo Ann Atcheson Gray

Contents

Into My Eyes
Poetry

Poem 1: Magic For Love

Magic For Love

Shimmers of light, with crystals so bright,

Sparkles of tears, joy just in sight.

Pinprick of blood from a fingertip,

That can only be tasted once upon the lip.

Dash of a crow's feather, so black,

Puff of smoke to simmer the pack.

A virgin's blood to seal the deal,

To make this magic seem so real.

Soft words spoken in a trance,

With a witch's eyelash to have a chance.

The magic is complete, pure perfection,

For love to show in a magical projection.

Magical love to show the way,

To the heart, who has gone astray.
Breathe easy, the task is done.
Affection and desire have already won.

Poem 2: The Vampire's Kiss

The Vampire's Kiss

Quietly. Cold. Seduction takes hold.

Lost in the vastness of secrets untold.

His kiss, his eternal lust,

Closes my eyes, leaving nothing but dust.

Taste of blood, a bitter delight,

As darkness fades away the light.

Lost in this numbness, so faint,

This kiss, this vampire, isn't a saint.

The warm blood, painful upon my lips,

As the vampire takes his final sip.

No more reality, all is unknown,

For all eternity is unnaturally shown.

Poem 3: Darkness

Darkness

No sight. Mere blackness.

Feeling alone and shattered,

Within this vastness.

Darkness all but tattered,

As one's life doesn't seem to matter.

Poem 4: Mystic Gem

Mystic Gem

A gem so bright, so magical,

Holds the power inside.

Red as a ruby, it couldn't be practical,

A curse that will not hide.

The heart strives for peace,

As the gem holds no release.

Only love can place the crack,

With the gem not holding back.

Power of decision to be made,

To break the gem by love,

A choice from a broken heart stayed,

Only the power coming from above.

A gem no longer withheld,

For love can conquer all.

Leaving the crack impaled,

With the heart never again behind a wall.

Poem 5: 'Broken'

'Broken'

Feeling lost, feeling numb.

Pain is real, no matter the cost.

Searching for the love, I lost.

No sight beyond this abyss,

Life flows on, no matter the risk.

Broken inside without you near,

Heart ceases to beat, love is gone.

Poem 6: Blood Sacrifice

Blood Sacrifice

Dark moon rises, gray clouds thicken,

A dagger taken; the blood revealed.

Weakness begins to quicken,

Sealing the bloody, vicious deal.

Heartbeat ceases to beat,

As darkness shadows over reality.

No more feeling, no more heat,

The coldness sets into one's insanity.

Poem 7: Blood of a Vampire

Blood of a Vampire
Blood runs cold as ice within my veins,
Flowing like a river, never to drain.
Never to love, never to feel,
Eternity for one such as I, is real.

Loneliness within this vastness,
Closes my eyes to my reality,
As this blood runs through with fastness,
Finding the blood of a vampire,
Isn't just formality.

Poem 8: Vampire's Seduction

Vampire's Seduction

Her kiss is cold upon my lips,

As my body warms my blood.

Her touch is ice upon my hips,

As desire comes in like a flood.

Her fangs pierce my neck,

As my pain is only brief.

The blood flows out like a wreck,

As my body weakens as a thief.

Darkness falls all around,

As life is slowly draining.

Feeling no longer abounds,

As my blood is never refraining.

Poem 9: Red Rose

Red Rose

Take this rose, red as fire,

Drop it into the soil, my deepest desire.

Lying in the darkness, voices I only hear,

Saying goodbyes as I shed a tear.

Left alone in this silence,

Only this red rose I hold as guidance.

Closing my eyes, I know it's real,

Death appears to come, no matter the deal.

Drifting into the vast unknown,

No shadows around to call my own.

Knowing this fate, I cannot heal it,

As I hold this red rose, I can no longer feel it.

Poem 10: Lady

Lady
The lady closes her eyes to what is seen,
Her need to rise is far from in between.
Blessings fly away within the clouds,
As she screams for love entirely too loud.

Eternity is all that lies in the distance,
If only it could really exist in an instant.
Darkness closes into one's own heart,
As she expresses her pain through such art.

Poem 11: Candle

Candle
Flame burning bright as the sun,
Flickering as the wax runs slow.
Darkness surrounds the fun,
As the candle gets too low.

Barely a hint of light,
As the night takes control.
Candle deems 'good night',
As the flame is no more bold.

Poem 12: The Perfect Funeral

The Perfect Funeral

Red roses strolled all around,

As I lay in my pearl, white coffin, silently.

Tears of sadness abound,

As words are spoken perfectly.

White satin dress covers my body,

As I hear dirt thrown vaguely,

The music stops, silence is hardy,

Darkness that tells me, it's gravely.

A red rose I hold near my chest,

No light to see the thorn,

I close my eyes as if to rest,

No feeling, only numb, I am torn.

Poem 13: Into My Eyes

Into My Eyes

Shadows peer unseen to one's desire,

Glimpse of darkness, light to my fire.

Into my eyes, stories untold,

Of dangers that are ages old.

Sadness deems around all corners,

As flashes of light become,

Such a border.

Into my eyes, you'll get lost,

Blinded by pain that wasn't,

A total loss.

Poem 14: "Eternity"

"Eternity"
Never dying, never crying,
Feeling a vast loneliness,
Longing for peace while trying,
To fill my undead heart with happiness.

Eternity is such a cruel word,
To walk this earth alone.
Never ceasing of things heard,
As I continue into the unknown.

Poem 15: 'The Ocean'

'The Ocean'
Waves brutal, yet calm,
Sand between your toes.
All worries fade away.

Birds fly overhead going astray,
As the wind blows.
The ocean rages on and on,
As all your cares seem small.

Poem 16: Angel's Wings

Angel's Wings

Wings so fierce, so wide, open for only a few to see.

Heavenly bliss to share, never to flee.

Protects you through the darkest of nights.

Always prepared for whatever the fight.

Shields one from the dimmest of light,

Until one is prepared for such a flight.

Poem 17: Walking Away

Walking Away
The sadness lingers mentally,
Decision must be made.
Should one stay or eventually,
Should one go, never to be repaid?

Fate can be cruel to one,
Destiny, leaving you undone.
Reality turns from fantasy,
As walking away, has won.

Poem 18: Niece

Niece
Adorable child with braids,
Like a daughter with an attitude,
Eyerolls, every time she aides,
Showing vaguely her gratitude.
Love unconditionally to give,
As she smiles with eyes of brown,
Knowing only happiness to live,
Never allowing her to frown.
Keeping her safe and sound,
As she grows into a wonderful lady,
Only success for life abounds,
Proudly, admitting my niece is never shady.

(Dedicated to my niece, Tracy)

Poem 19: Undone

Undone

The vastness.
Can't be undone.
The sacredness.
Will leave you undone.
Loneliness.
Everyone is undone.
The hurtfulness.
The heart is undone.
Spirituality.
The soul is undone.
Reality. Fantasy.
Is never undone.

Poem 20: A Vampire's Tear

A Vampire's Tear

Blood drips from my eye,

The pain ceases from my heart.

I no longer feel,

I only express through art.

This blood tear falls from my cheek,

As I throw this canvas into the creek.

Memories to bury, to drown,

Never again to resurface the pain I unbound.

A blood tear falls once more,

As I let go, accepting nevermore.

Poem 21: The Heart

The Heart

Ask me how I knew.
Ask me how I know.
Ask me when we're through.
And I will tell you no.

Poem 22: Fearful Immortal

Fearful Immortal

Your eyes are hollow,

Your pain is deep.

Blood flows in your veins,

Yet its color you cannot keep.

Darkness is your light,

Yet it holds your heart tight.

Eternity is far away,

For one such affright.

Poem 23: Love Dies

Love Dies

Darkness creeps in.
Night.
Silence is deafening.
Love Ends.
Shadows start to stir.
Heart ceases to feel.
Love Ends.
Eternity awaits.
Darkness creeps in.
Love Ends.

Poem 24: 'Friend'

'Friend'

Sheds a tear for your pain,

Holds your hand through the loss,

Stands with you within the rain,

Cries placed upon the shoulder.

A friend overstays their welcome,

Happily, shares the secrets,

Haunting your mind with what is right or wrong,

Showing love without anything to gain.

Though apart, but never alone,

Prayers exceed to what is not known.

Eternity may never exist,

But a friend will never resist.

Poem 25: Beauty Fades

Beauty Fades

Bitter love eternal,
If only, you submit now.
Death to all feelings as human,
Only you can make such a vow.

Just a touch of pain,
With so much more to gain.
Eternity awaits for you,
A sacrifice well over-due.

Poem 26: 'Awaken'

'Awaken'

Petals of the rarest rose,

To scent the flame,

The blackest hair unfroze,

To allow no one to blame.

Blood of a virgin to seal,

The fire shines brightly,

As the ritual closes the deal,

Not to mistaken, its power lightly.

Making the ritual complete,

Once the blood of the virgin,

Has dripped to one's feet.

Reality fades away to darkness,

Leaving the mind to flee.

It has awakened.

Poem 27: Dark Art

Dark Art

The canvas comes alive with rage,
Reds, blacks, color of whatever age.
Her demons come to light all along the page,
Singing the song of her ending of days.

Into My Eyes
Poetry

By: Anna Elizabeth
Jo Ann Atcheson Gray

Thanks

Thank you!

Hope you enjoyed this little book of dark poetry!!

Jo Ann